HISTORY CORNER

World War Two

Stephen White-Thomson

Explore the world with **Popcorn** - your complete first non-fiction library.

Look out for more titles in the Popcorn range. All books have the same format of simple text and striking images. Text is carefully matched to the pictures to help readers to identify and understand key vocabulary. www.waylandbooks.co.uk/popcorn

Published in paperback in 2014 by Wayland
Copyright © Wayland 2014

Wayland
Hachette Children's Books
338 Euston Road
London NW1 3BH

Wayland Australia
Level 17/207 Kent Street
Sydney NSW 2000

 Produced for Wayland by
White-Thomson Publishing Ltd
www.wtpub.co.uk
+44 (0)843 208 7460

Editor: Stephen White-Thomson
Designer: Clare Nicholas
Picture researcher: Stephen White-Thomson
Series consultant: Kate Ruttle
Design concept: Paul Cherrill

British Library Cataloguing in Publication Data
White-Thomson, Stephen.
   World War II. -- (History corner)(Popcorn)
   1. World War, 1939-1945--Juvenile literature.
   I. Title II. Series
   940.5'4-dc23

ISBN: 978 0 7502 8340 3

Wayland is a division of Hachette Children's Books,
an Hachette UK company.
www.hachette.co.uk

Printed and bound in China

10 9 8 7 6 5 4 3 2 1

Picture/illustration credits:
Corbis: David Pollack/Corbis 7, Hulton-Deutsch Collection 10-11, 12, Corbis 16, Poodlesrock/Corbis 19; Getty: Hulton Archive/Stringer 4-5, IWM/Getty Images 8-9, Getty Images 13, 14, 17, SSPL via Getty Images 15, Popperfoto/Getty 18; Shutterstock Atlaspix/Shutterstock title page, mrHanson/Shutterstock.com 6, V. J. Matthew/Shutterstock.com 20, Bikeworldtravel/Shutterstock.com 21; Peter Bull Illustration 23 Cover tbc

Every effort has been made to clear copyright.
Should there be any inadvertent omission,
please apply to the publisher for rectification.

 Contents

World at war

World War Two was called a
world war because so many
countries joined in. It lasted
six years, from 1939 to 1945.

A13·13

Countries like Russia, America and Britain were on one side. We call them the Allies. The main countries on the other side were Germany and Japan.

More than 1.7 billion people and 61 countries were in the war.

PA 3-27

60 million people were killed during the war.

The war begins

Adolf Hitler was the German leader. Germany had been defeated in World War One. Hitler wanted Germany to be a powerful country again.

Adolf Hitler was the leader of the Nazis.

This stamp shows Adolf Hitler in 1939, the year World War Two started.

Hitler's armies invaded countries next to Germany. Britain and France told him to stop. Hitler did not stop, so the war against Germany began on 3 September 1939.

Winston Churchill was Britain's leader for most of the war.

"LET US GO FORWARD TOGETHER"

Dunkirk

In 1940, the Germans invaded France. They trapped British and French soldiers in a small town by the sea called Dunkirk.

Hundreds of big and small British boats made many trips across the sea. They carried soldiers from the beaches in Dunkirk in France safely back to England.

German bomber aeroplanes attacked British troops as they waited to be rescued.

9

Battle of Britain

Hitler wanted to win the war.
He tried to weaken the British.
He sent over many German
planes to bomb their cities.

British and German planes fought fierce battles. This is called the Battle of Britain. The British won, but some German planes did reach the cities.

British pilots run towards their aeroplanes to fight the Germans in the air.

11

The Blitz and evacuation

Between September 1940 and May 1941, German planes dropped bombs on British cities. This was called the Blitz. Two million homes were destroyed.

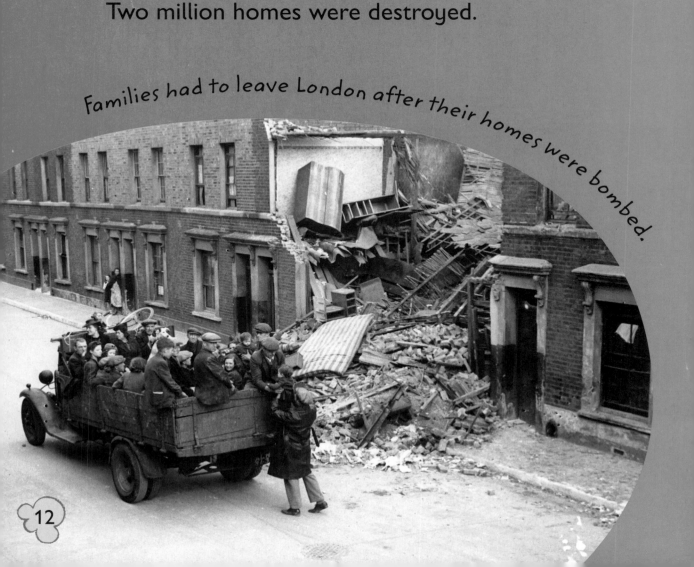

Families had to leave London after their homes were bombed.

It was too dangerous for children to stay in the cities. They left their homes and went to stay in the countryside. This is called evacuation.

Evacuees wait at a railway station.

Children wore labels with their names and addresses on them.

Rationing

There was less food during the war. People were given ration books with coupons inside them. They had to swap the coupons for food in the shops.

In 1943, eggs were rationed to only four a month.

People grew their own food.

Clothes were also rationed.
People were told to keep old
clothes and to mend them.

This poster
asks people to
mend their
clothes and
keep their
old pots
and pans.

MEND AND
MAKE-DO
TO SAVE
BUYING NEW

MAKE-DO
AND MEND

PRINTED FOR H.M. STATIONERY OFFICE BY W. R. ROYLE & SON, LTD. 51 3721

ISSUED BY THE BOARD OF TRADE

Women and war

Women could not fight in the army.
They did jobs that men normally did.
Many joined the Women's Land Army
and worked hard on farms.

This poster shows that women could do tough jobs as well as men.

Women worked in factories where they made bombs and helped to build aeroplanes and tanks. They also mended trucks and motorbikes.

When she was a princess during the war, Queen Elizabeth mended trucks.

Women work on a fighter aeroplane.

The war ends

Britain, America and Russia made a final attack on Germany. On 8 May 1945, Germany surrendered. The Allies celebrated VE (Victory in Europe) Day.

Soldiers were welcomed home as heroes.

It took longer to defeat Japan,
but on 15 August 1945 Japan
surrendered. The Allies celebrated
VJ (Victory in Japan) Day.

American planes bombed Japan to make it surrender.

Remembering

People were happy that the war had ended, but 60 million people had died during the war. People were very sad, and they were very tired.

This war memorial in Canada helps us remember soldiers who died in the war.

On Remembrance Day every
11 November, we remember
the people who died during
World War Two and other wars.

Women in World War Two uniforms march through
London every year on Remembrance Day.

World War Two quiz

What have you found out about World War Two?
Can you match the event or person in the panel
with the sentences below?

a. Battle of Britain   b. Blitz   c. Churchill

d. Dunkirk   e. Hitler   f. VE Day

1. The leader of the German Nazis.

2. The British leader during the war.

3. The name of the French town from which the
   Allied army was rescued in 1940.

4. When Allied pilots won an air fight against
   the Germans.

5. The bombing of British cities from September 1940
   to May 1941.

6. The name given to the day when victory in
   Europe was won.

Make an eggless cake

Eggs were rationed during World War Two. People used this recipe to make cakes during the war.

1. Sieve the flour and salt into basin, then rub in the margarine. Add the currants, sultanas, fruit peel and sugar. Mix well.

2. Dissolve the saccharin tablets in a dessert spoonful of hot water. Add them to the milk and water, then beat them into the flour mixture. Put mixture into a baking tin that has been greased and dusted with flour.

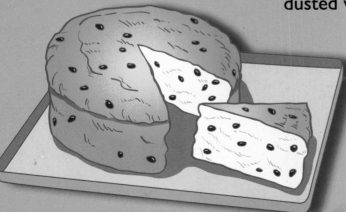

3. Bake for 1½ hours in a hot oven (180°C) on the middle shelf. Yummy!

Glossary

Allies the countries who fought with the British

army a large group of people who are trained to fight on land in a war

attack to attack someone means to fight them and hurt them

Blitz the bombing of Britain between September 1940 and May 1941

bomb a weapon that explodes and hurts people or damages things

celebrate to do something special on an important day

defeat if you defeat someone, you beat them in a game or battle

evacuee someone who travels from their home in a dangerous place to live in a safer place

invade to go into another country to take it over

Nazis the political party led by Adolf Hitler

pilot someone who flies an aeroplane

rationing if you ration something (food, clothes), you get less of it

rescue if you rescue someone, you save them from danger

surrender when people surrender, they stop fighting and give themselves up

tanks heavy trucks that are used in war and move on metal tracks

trapped you are trapped when you cannot get away from somewhere

war memorial something that it built to remember soldiers who have died in wars

Index